This Book Belongs To:

_____

_____

Aa 1 Bb 2

Note from the Publisher

We hope that you have a lot of fun watching your little one color in their *Toddler Coloring Book*! Let the friendly lion lead the way to new skills and coordination, as your child covers the page with their colors of choice. (Most pages are single sided to avoid bleed-through.)

Let your toddler go at their own pace, gradually getting better at coloring inside the lines. Associating letters, words, numbers, and colors together will start them off on a great learning path. This coloring book is designed to engage creativity and encourage learning at the same time. Many thanks to Katie, Haisley, Cassidy, and Maddie for their help in drawing the illustrations! And thanks to Frank Oliver for his help with the wonderful cover design.

Please let us know how you and your little one enjoy the book - pictures are most welcome in our Review section on the Product Page. Happy Coloring!

Lily Kim, author

Ladybug

Starfish

Lion

Giraffe

Cow

Tiger

Hippo

Bear

Beaver

Dinosaur

Bat

Gorilla

Crab

Octopus

Pony

Bunny

Butterfly

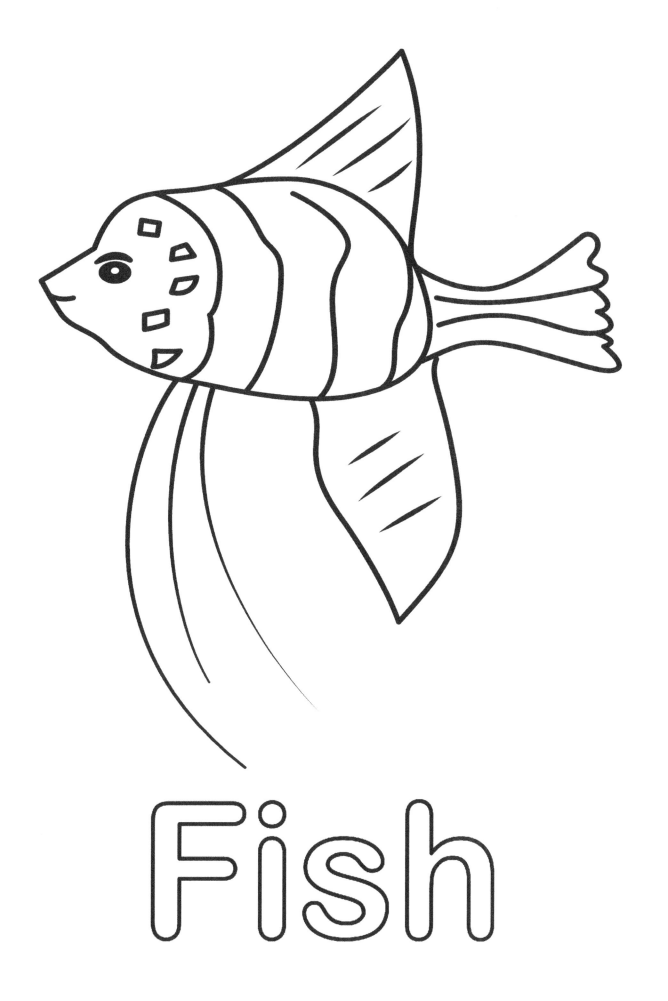

Fish

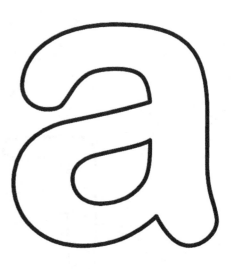

Apple

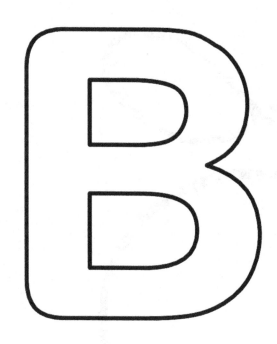
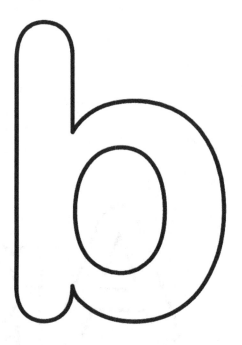

Balloons

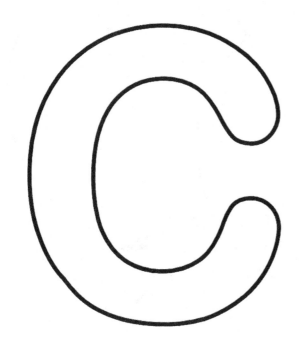

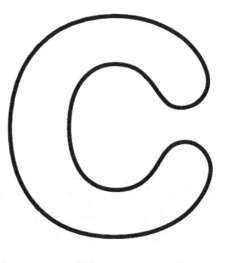

Cat

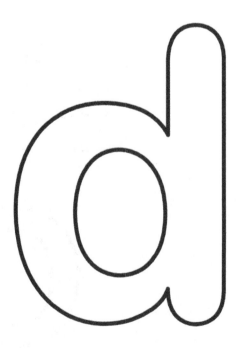

Dog

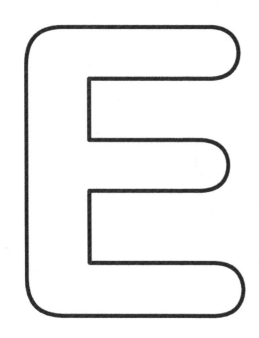
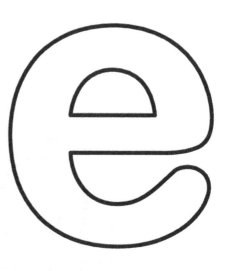

Elephant

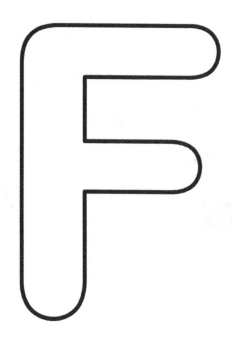

Frog

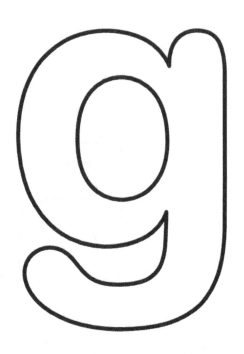

Grapes

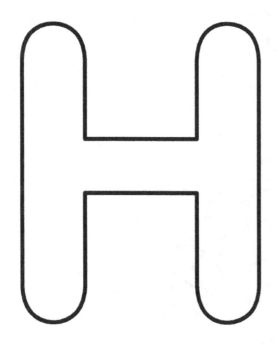

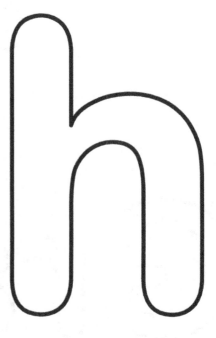

House

Insect

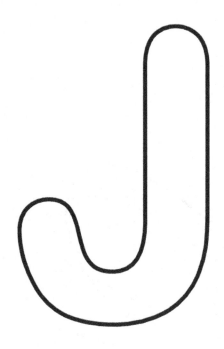

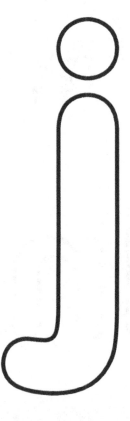

Jellyfish

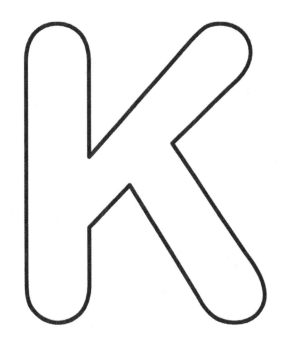

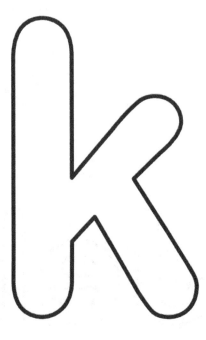

Kangaroo

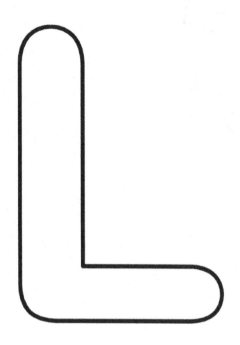

Lamb

Mouse

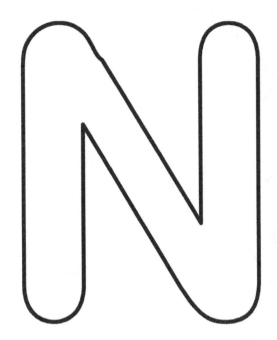

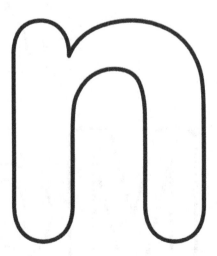

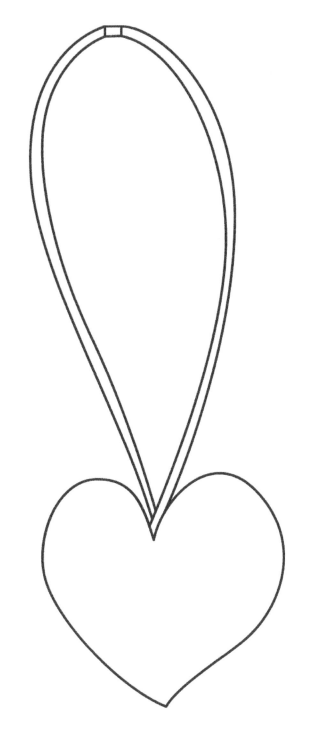

Necklace

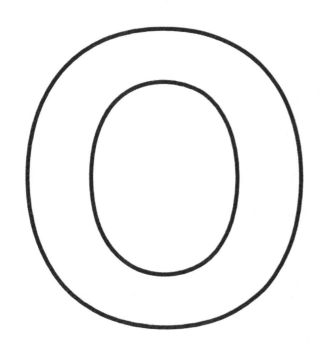

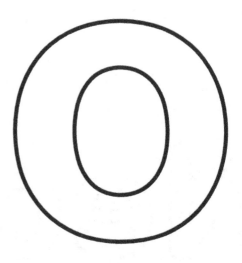

Owl

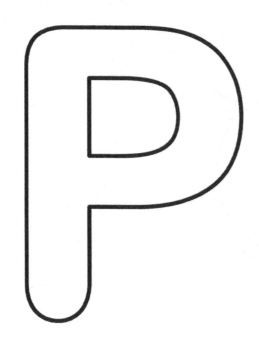

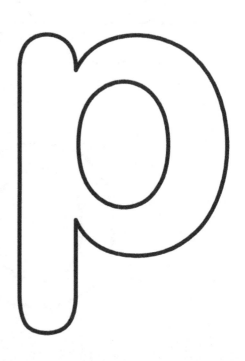

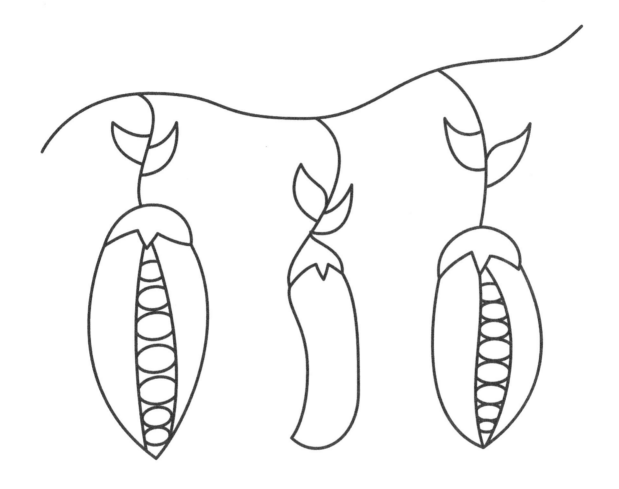

Peas

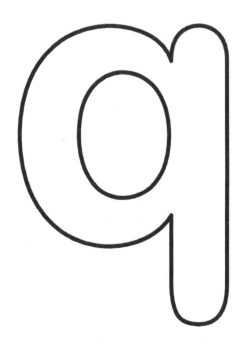

Quail

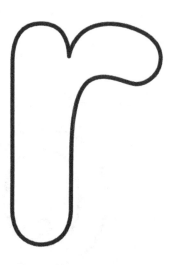

Rainbow

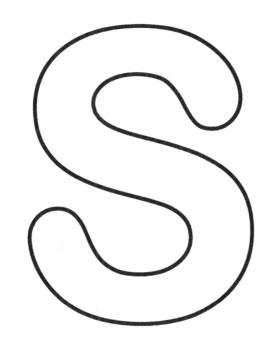

S

Snail

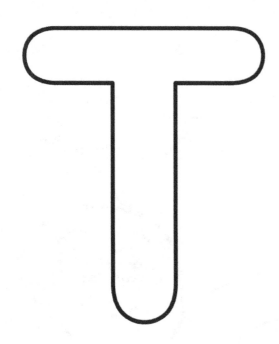

Turtle

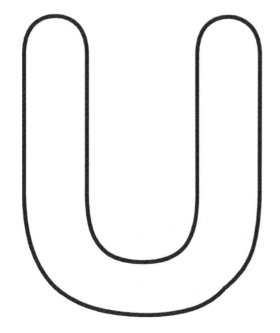

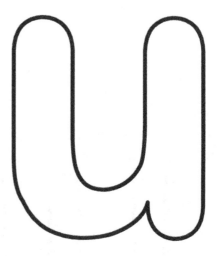

Umbrella

Violin

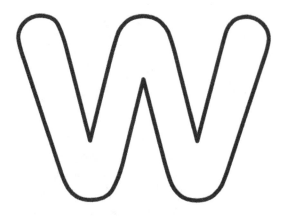

Whale

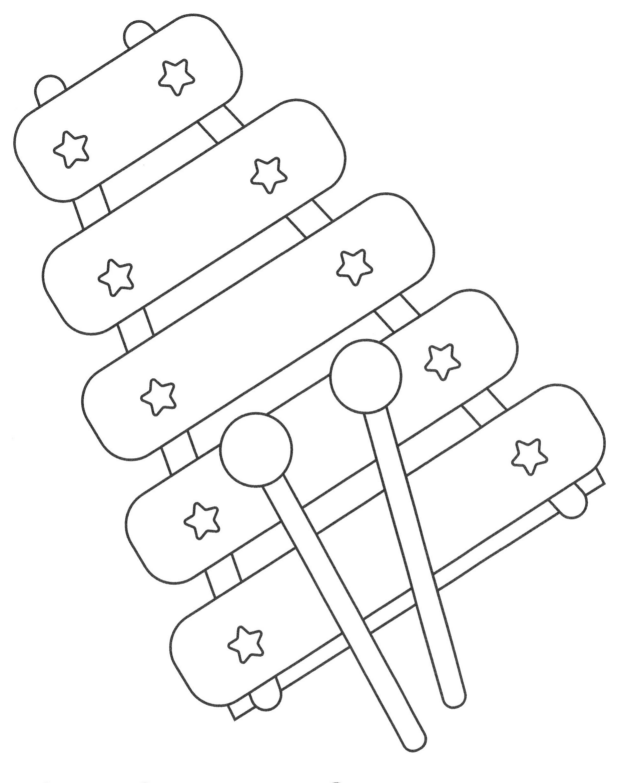

Xylophone

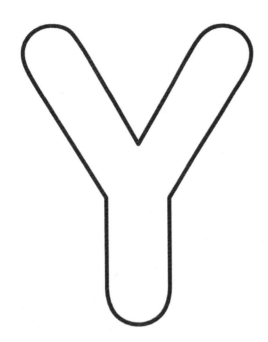

Yak

Z z

Zebra

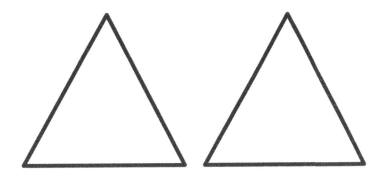

3

★★★

Three

4

Four

5

Five

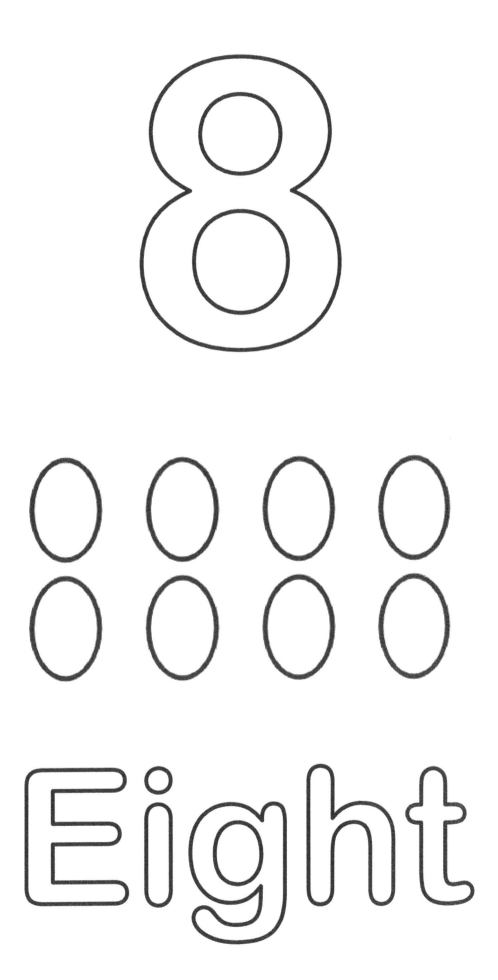

10

Ten

Made in the USA
Monee, IL
21 December 2023

50315783R00070